C Programming

C Programming Language for beginners, teaching you how to learn to code in C fast!

Table of Contents

Introduction

Thank you for taking the time to pick up this book: C Programming.

This book covers the topic of C Programming, what it is, and what you can do with C programming.

You will learn how to do basic commands in C language, and discover how to begin programming in C. You will also learn about the history of programming, and discover what doors that learning 'C' can open for you!

At the completion of this book you will have a good understanding of how C Programming works and should have a great foundation for becoming a fantastic programmer in C!

This beginner's guide will give you a great start in your programming journey, and provide a powerful foundation for any subsequent language you choose to learn!

Once again, thanks for reading this book, I hope you find it to be helpful!

Chapter 1:
What is Programming?

For those that do not know, programming languages are written code that instruct a computer to perform actions. Ultimately a computer can only interpret 1's and 0's, but giving instructions that way is cumbersome and difficult. Low-level programming languages map processor instructions to words that can be translated to binary, but even low-level languages are hard to understand. High-level programming languages are a way to use near-natural English to program computers.

Programming is a rewarding hobby and lucrative career field where an individual does not need a degree to prove their knowledge- reading books such as this can provide the same level of education that a college class can. As the world integrates technology more into our everyday lives, programmers will be more and more needed for their talents. Intelligent individuals will enjoy the challenge that comes from learning a programming language.

What is the C language?

C is a third-generation computer programming language first developed by Dennis Ritchie and Brian Kernighan in the late 1960's and early 1970's. The language was used to rewrite UNIX in 1972, and it has since become one of the most widespread and influential programing languages in the history of computing.

A Very Short Synopsis on the History of Programming

The first configurable computers were often programed without the use of a programing language. Early computer programs had to be manually written in machine code, and they were read from paper punch cards, magnetic tape, or even by toggling switches by hand. For these antiquated computers the early methods of early computer programming are called *first-generation programming languages* or simply *1GL*.

History's next iteration of programing languages, termed as *second-generation programming languages or 2GL*, contained the first implementation of assembly language. This made computer programs more readable to computer programmers and alleviated the tedium of writing.

The last generation of programing languages (that we will discuss), are known as *third-generation programing languages or 3GL*, and were first written in the 1950's. Nearly all 3GL high-level computer programming languages were far more programmer friendly and machine independent than their predecessors - this is the generation of programming languages that C falls into.

The History of the C Programming Language

C is the successor to programming language B, which was developed at Bell Labs in 1969.

Work on C began in 1972 as a language that could fix B's shortcomings and serve a niche market. C was useful enough, though, that it was ported to a multitude of systems and thus became relatively widespread. UNIX is an operating system that was popular at the time, and the usability of C led to a rewrite of the OS. UNIX and thus C were then used in computer systems all over the country.

Brain Kernighan and Dennis Ritchie published the first edition of *The C Programming Language* in 1978- a book with a recognizable cover that taught programmers everywhere how to use C. Different versions of C continued to exist until the early 1980's when the ANSI group standardized a version of C that became known as Standard C, C89, or ANSI C. ANSI C is the same version of C that was commonly learned in universities and integrated into embedded computer systems. The early 1990's saw the updated C90; later implementations were standardized as C99. Finally, the newest version of C was released in 2011 with the name C11. Each iteration of the C language brought new functionality and additional improvements over efficiency and design. This book will focus on the BLANK standard, as it is the most commonly used.

C's prevalent nature as in influential language is marked by the sheer number of other languages that have C as a pedigree. C++, C#, Python, Java, Perl, and various other languages take queues from C's structure, which is why C is considered with such high regard.

What the C Programming Language is used for

C has been used as a general, all-purpose programming language for many years. Anything imaginable can and has been written using C, such as operating systems, text editors, computer games, multimedia players, and more. Operating systems such as Microsoft Windows, Mac's OSX, as well as

Linux kernel based operating systems like Ubuntu, Debian, and Google's Android are all written using the C programming language in some way.

The reason that C is so widely used is due to the portability of code, its efficiency, and C's ability to access the specific addresses of hardware, its ability of type punning, and its very low run-time demand on system resources.

Why You Should Learn to Program in C

The programming language C has been in existence for decades, and it will continue to thrive for decades to come. There is a massive amount of source code obtainable freely that you can utilize in your own programs, and online help for C is unmatched. Newer language's pedigrees are usually traced back to C, so learning how to program starting with C will give an ingrained advantage when studying alternative ones. The powerful functions contained within the language are a fantastic mix between high-level, natural text and low-level technical jargon. The portability of C gives it a large advantage over pure assembly language, because multiple processor types are compatible with C and it can therefore run on many systems.

Chapter 2:
Getting Started

How Programs are Written

Just as with other Algorithmic Languages (ALGOL), C is a facilitator of structured programing. This means that the nature of the language promotes clarity of code, and reduces the time of developing programs. Programming in C for Windows requires an Integrated Development Environment (IDE). Code is written in an IDE much in the same way it is written in a text editor, but IDEs offer great bonus features such as syntax highlighting and numbered lines that are designed specifically for programmers to take advantage of. Written code must be compiled, or built, which is the act of translating our high-level C code into lower-level machine code that the computer can understand. "Built" is the simple definition of a 5-step process that early coders had to do manually but IDEs handle for us automatically quite well.

1. Preprocessing - <include> statements and libraries are processed and loaded to be used in the source code.

2. Compiling – the programmer's source code is expanded with the preprocessing statements and compiled into assembly code.

3. Assembly – the assembly code is processed further closer to computer-understandable machine code.

4. Linking – the final, runnable executable is formed by packaging all the required materials into a single source that the computer can run.

5. Loading – the program is run, and the code executes.

After compilation, which can take a long time for large programs, the code can be run.

Code::Blocks, a Free and Easy IDE

Code::Blocks is a free and open source cross-platform IDE that supports a wide variety of programming languages, including C. The IDE contains and can support many compilers to ensure that running code is only a 1-click process. One great feature of Code::Blocks is its syntax highlighting. This means that the color of certain elements will change colors based on what that element is. This makes navigating your code even easier. Code::Blocks also enables the use of code folding, meaning that you can "fold" or "roll up" sections of code for ease of navigation purposes. Code::Blocks also features a debugger that processes full breakpoint support. Overall, Code:Blocks is a helpful IDE for the beginning programmer on Windows.

Installing the Code::Blocks IDE is relatively simple. After going to the download page of http://codeblocks.org, you can download the binary releases of Code::Blocks for Microsoft Windows XP, Vista, 7, 8, and Windows 10. Support also exists for i386 Linux machines, amd64 Linux machines, and Mac OS X. Alternatively, if your Linux machine is supports APT, you can use the command "apt-get install codeblocks", or "sudo apt-get install codeblocks" on Ubuntu operating systems. It is not common, however to use an IDE on a UNIX based system, as most programmers prefer to use something called the "toolchain" that is already built in to Linux-based and OSX-based operating systems. We will discuss this more in depth later. Launch the installer and install everything.

Now that you have Code::Blocks installed, start the application. You will be asked to select a default compiler. Do not worry if you only have one compiler available, as the default GNU GCC will compile our C programs that we write in this book. If you are on a Windows machine that has never had a compiler installed, nothing will show on the list, so you will have to download one manually (https://sourceforge.net/projects/tdm-gcc/files/TDM-GCC%20Installer/tdm-gcc-5.1.0-3.exe/download). Install the compiler with all options enabled and restart Code::Blocks selecting the now installed compiler.

Of course, Code::Blocks actually offers a download version with a compiler built in, and that is the most recommended option. On the IDE download page just select the one with "minGW" in the name.

Creating a Project

Creating a C project in Code::Blocks involves a few steps. Upon startup, you will be greeted with a start screen. Clicking "create new project" is the first stop here. We will be working within the console, so click "console application", and then "C". Name the project, give it a location, select our GCC compiler, and then the files will be created. In the left window open the tab for sources and you should see our main script file, main.c. Double click it to open it in the middle panel, and we can see a program already set up for us. You type code into this window, and build it with some of the toolbar buttons at the top. Let us go ahead and run the default program here. On the top toolbar look for a play button with a gear symbol that stands for "build and run". So long as the compiler is installed correctly and the code is correct, you should see "Hello, World!" in a black console window.

Coding in Linux

Linux-based operating systems are known for their ease-of-use when it comes to programming and coding. Before graphical user interfaces were popular on computers, text-only operating systems such as UNIX had programmers coding in much the same way Linux and OSX systems do now. No additional components are needed to start coding in Linux, not even an IDE as every tool is built in to the most popular distros.

That is why experienced programmers (and this book) recommend programming on Linux. Less things can go wrong, and setup is virtually nonexistent. You can either install a Linux-based OS such as Ubuntu alongside your current Windows OS, or you could run Linux within a virtual machine using VirtualBox. Granted, the following steps are optional, but any serious programmer is going to be using Linux as some point anyways so it's recommended to get a start early.

To install Ubuntu alongside Windows, download an .iso file from http://www.ubuntu.com/download/desktop. Ubuntu is free, so you don't have to pay for the download. Next, get a program that can write image files to external drives such as https://rufus.akeo.ie/. You will also need an empty USB drive. Plug in the drive, backup any data you had on it, and start the Rufus program. Select the Ubuntu ISO and start the writing process. When it finishes shut down the computer and boot into BIOS with an "F" key. Change the startup order to check external drives first, save and then quit. The computer should boot from the removable media and start Ubuntu. From the "Live CD" you could begin programming right away, or you could also install the OS so the USB is not needed. Double clicking the install icon on the desktop will prompt the user for options, so be sure to select "install alongside Windows". When it is done your computer will be dual-booting two different operating systems, and you will be able to choose between them on power-on.

For those that do not wish to install Ubuntu entirely, using a virtual machine application such as VirtualBox can quickly provide a Linux programming environment. Download an Ubuntu image (32-bit is recommended for a virtual OS) and the VirtualBox application from https://www.virtualbox.org/wiki/Downloads. Install the program and create a virtual machine, adhering to all prompts. Direct the program to the Ubuntu image and you should be able to boot into Ubuntu while already being booted into Windows.

Regardless of your method of running Linux, here is how we will create our default hello world script. Start a terminal (either search for it, double click it, ctrl+shift+T, or ctrl+alt+T). First we will create a new folder for programming, so type *mkdir Programming*. This creates a new folder. Type *cd Programming* to change directories to the new folder. Within this folder we can type *ls* to list files, but there will be none since we have created none. Through the program nano we are given a simple text editor that has IDE functions such as syntax highlighting. Just type *nano test.c* to create a new C file (where test is replaced by your project name).

Nano will show a blank prompt where you are free to type your program. The following text is the basic hello world program that we will be referring to subsequently. Type it in exactly being careful to not misspell anything – accuracy is required for programming!

```
#include <stdio.h>

int main()

{

    printf("Hello, World!\n");

    return 0;

}
```

After writing it all down, press ctrl+x to quit nano. It will ask if you'd like to save changes first, so key "y" for yes. You will return to the terminal back in the "Programming" folder, and now that we have written our source code we will need to compile it.

```
gcc test.c
```

The above terminal command will use the GNU gcc compiler to go through 4 of the 5 compiling steps and output a file "a.out" in the current directory. A.out is the default output name, put you can specify the built file by adding some options to the command.

```
gcc test.c −o test
```

Which will output "test" instead. The final step is to run the program. Typing "./a.out" for the default file name or "./test" for the renamed one will start running the built executable. The period tells Linux to "run" and the /filename is the file to run. On the screen you should see the fruits of your labor, "Hello, World!".

The next chapter will break down what we've typed in so we can really get started with learning how to program!

Chapter 3:
Breaking Down How to Program

How Hello World Works

As you may have already noticed, programming code in this book is italicized to indicate itself. Depending on the format that you are reading this book in, the carefully formatted code might be placed strangely or look incorrect. Firstly, you should note that formatting is completely disregarded in C, as whitespace and tabs are eliminated. Do not worry too much about the placement of commands as you copy them, for they only need to be on their own lines. Formatting is just for human readability.

Now we will break down what each part of the hello world program does. The first line is here:

#include <stdio.h>

And that is called a preprocessor statement. #include tells the compiler that the specified file will need to be built into the compiled executable in order to provide the functionality necessary to run the program. Stdio.h is a file that provides standard input and output (Standard Input Output) commands such as the printf() used later in the program, and it is very much needed for just about any program we write in this book- never forget to include it.

int main()

{

These lines mark the beginning of our main function. Every bit of code between the curly brackets will run when a C program is executed. The *'int'* is unimportant right now, and so is the parenthesis. Just know that this is how you specify where our code is.

printf("Hello, World!\n");

The printf() is our first real "command", and it tells the computer to print the message contained in quotations. "Hello, World!" will be displayed but the "\n" will not, because \n is a special case that signifies to start a new line. Any command or function will contain parenthesis, and the contents between them are known as arguments. There is only one argument in this function, but some commands have multiple arguments separated by commas. After the ending parenthesis there is a semicolon, which goes at the end of any command.

return 0;

}

This is our next command, which simply finishes execution of the program. Any number could go there, but 0 is the traditional value. Notice again that there is a semicolon because a command is being executed. Lastly there is the closing curly bracket, signifying that int main() is over.

While simple in theory, there is plenty going on in our simple beginner program. Try playing around with it by changing the text or using multiple printf() statements to type out more lines.

Commenting

Code can quickly become an alien language, especially when everything is new and confusing. C has a built-in feature that allows you to annotate code to help you better understand it – this is called a 'comment'. Within our code we can start typing a comment with:

```
//
```

Anything to the right of double slashes is ignored by the compiler, so we can use it to explicate upon our code.

```
printf("This is a test"); //this command displays a
```
message

As we will learn later it is good coding practice to comment on anything that is not obvious.

Chapter 4:
Beginner C Concepts – Variables, Input

Variables

Variables are pieces of data that store values and can change. Examples of variables include numbers, letters, properties, and events. A variable has a type, name, and a value, such as *int numberOfDogs* and *12,* but each variable must be created with at least a type and name for identification purposes. Their names must not start with a number or special symbols - only letters. Additionally, a variable's value must correspond to the declared data type, so an integer variable must contain numbers and so on. A few data types are discussed below.

Data Types	
Integers	Integers (int) are 4 byte variables that contain a whole number from blank to blank.
Floating Point Numbers	A *float* is a 4 byte variable that stands for decimal numbers from blank to blank.
Extended Precision Float	For cases where additional accuracy is needed a float can be declared extended by designating it an 8 byte *double*.
Character	Characters, designated *char*, are 1 byte variables that contain a single character (letter, number, or symbol). *Strings* are multiple characters combined to create a word or sentence.

Creating a Variable

Variables are declared, or created, through code in a declaration statement, and variables are given a value through assignment.

> *int var1;*

A statement such as the one above will create an integer with the name var1. Since var1 is an integer, it can contain a number. Therefore, we would use the following line to give var1 a value:

> *var1 = 10;*

With the first line in this section we declared an integer, and with the second we assigned the integer a value. But you do not need to first declare and then assign, for you can do both with a single initialization action.

> *float var2 = 2.3;*

Displaying a Variable

With the command printf() we can also display variables by using a "format specifier".

> *int var1 = 22;*

> *printf("var1 contains the number %d", var1);*

These lines of code display the specified variable by replacing the "%d" format specifier with the provided variable, var1. The format specifier varies depending on the data type, so %d works for integers, %f is for floats, %c gets replaced by characters, and %s exists for strings.

Manipulating Variables

Variables that have a datatype with numbers can be interacted with mathematically with a number of operators. The <stdio.h> header contains basic arithmetic, but <math.h> contains additional math functions such as square roots and trigonometric commands.

var1 = var1 - 2;

This assignment statement changes the value of var1 by performing subtraction and then updating the variable with the result. Multiple variables can be used in a single line to perform a complex function such as the one below. Note that the order of operations is followed

sum = var1 + (var3 − var1) // when var1 is initially 3 and var2 is initially 5, sum will contain 5 after the command runs

Variable manipulation with arithmetic is not just limited to addition and subtraction. The other operands multiplication (*), division (/), and modular division (%) can be used as well.

Obtaining Input for Variables

While printf() remains the best beginner's output method, input is best handled through the scanf() command.

scanf(input, variable);

Where *scanf("%d", &var1);* would prompt the user for input (%d) and assign it to var1 (the ampersand is required when inputting integers, but we will reference this later). The program lines below demonstrate the use of scanf() and how to use it effectively.

```
int age, ageInFive;

printf("What is your age?\n");

scanf("%d", &age);

ageInFive = age + 5;

printf("In five years you will be %d", ageInFive);
```

Bringing Everything Together with a Simple Arithmetic Program

```
//C Program for converting seconds into minutes

#include <stdio.h>

int main()

{

        int secondsInput, minutes, remainder;  //declare
variables

        printf("Convert seconds into minutes.\n");

        printf("Please enter the number of seconds: ");

        scanf("%d", &secondsInput);

        minutes = secondsInput / 60;  //find out the number of
minutes

        remainder = secondsInput % 60;  //find out the
leftover seconds
```

```
        printf("%d seconds is equal to %d minutes and %d
leftover seconds\n", secondsInput, minutes, remainder);

        return 0;

}
```

The opposite of a variable is a constant, a defined value that never changes through the course of a program. Because they cannot change, they are defined in a different way than variables as seen below:

```
int area;        //declaring a variable like normal

const float PI = 3.14; //declaring an unchangeable
constant with const
```

Using constants is good programming form, especially since they are never meant to change. Programming slip-ups or a mismanagement of memory can accidently change the value of a variable, but defining one as static and constant ensures it will not falter.

Conclusively, variables and constants are representations of data that can be numbers, letters, words, and so on. Variables can be manipulated through mathematical function, displayed to the screen, and received as input to create interactive programs.

Chapter 5:
Continued Beginner Concepts
– Strings, Conditionals

Working with Text Input

The char data type works much the same way that integers work, except that the typical char initialization is done with single quotes surrounding the value.

char choice = 'a';

Only a single character can be stored as a char, so words must be stored with multiple chars. Instead of declaring a variable for each letter in a word, though, we can use an array declaration to create a string. Consider the following:

char firstName[] = "Phillip";

What we've done is create an array of characters and assigned each letter of "Phillip" to another spot in the array. If displayed on the screen with *printf("String firstName = %s", firstName);*, then we would see "String name = Phillip" as each character in the array is displayed in succession. Broken down, the array would look like this.

P	H	I	L	L	I	P

And calling the specific array location will pull only the character requested, just as the command below prints only the first letter in the string to the screen (remembering that programmers start counting with 0).

printf("First letter in firstName = %c", firstName[0]);

Finally, strings have their own header file <string.h> that can be used to provide more commands- the most useful of which being strcpy(). Placing one string in the first argument of the command will fill the string with the contents of the second argument.

strcpy(firstName, "Jack");

Where the above would replace Phillip with Jack as the firstName variable.

strcpy(firstName, lastName);

And where this command would replace the firstName with the lastName. Assigning contents to strings outside of declaration statements sometimes requires using strcpy(); always be sure to include the <string.h> header file when working with string commands.

Arrays in Detail

Arrays are used to keep variables neat and organized. As it is seen previously, arrays are specified with square brackets while initializing a variable. Empty brackets create a dynamically sized array, but you can also specify a number to create a fixed size array.

int grades[5] = {87, 92, 40, 100, 73};

printf("%d", grades[3]);

Notice that strings can be printed fully with %s, but integers must be displayed individually through printf().

The advantage gained through using arrays exists from the fact that only one variable is needed for any subset of numbers. This can save space and help organize variables better in programs.

Conditional Statements

The best programs offer interactivity to the user. Given that our first C programs have limited interactivity, the usefulness of our applications are also constrained. Conditional statements are a way to offer "multiple paths" to a user through comparisons and conditions. Let us break down this programming snippet.

```
printf("Please enter your test grade.\n");

scanf("%d", testGrade);

if (testGrade >= 90) {

        printf("You have an A.");

}

if (testGrade < 90) {

        printf("You do not have an A.");

}
```

The program receives a testGrade from the user and begins the first conditional statement. In the first check, testGrade is compared against 90, and if the number is indeed greater than everything within that, the statement's braces is performed. If the condition is not met than the entire braces are skipped.

A value of 70 for testGrade will not fulfil the first comparison, so it will not be performed. It does, however, meet the second comparison; the console will print back "You do not have an A" to the user.

Conditional statements are performed through comparisons such as the ones above, and there are various operators through which comparisons can be made.

Comparison Operators		
Operator	**Meaning**	**Example**
==	"is equal to"	if (userAge == 21)
>	"is greater than"	if (userAge > 20)
<	"is less than"	if (userAge < 22)
>=	"is greater than or equal to"	if (userAge >= 21)
<=	"is less than or equal to"	if (userAge <= 21)
!=	"is not equal to"	if (userAge != 40)

Moreover, multiple comparisons can be made with more operators.

Conditional Comparison Operators		
Operator	**Meaning**	**Example**
&&	"and if"	if (userAge >= 20 && testScore == 100)
||	"or if"	If (userAge == 12 || userAge == 21)

Bringing it all Together in an Input-Conditional Program

Using 'if' statements can open up numerous programming possibilities in C. However, even though 'if' statements are very useful, making multiple redundant 'if' comparisons is actually a bad programming practice. Programmers should instead take advantage of the other conditional keywords available to them (else if, else). We can improve our grading program from above to further explain how else and else if work.

//Program to translate a grade into a mark.

#include <stdio.h>

int main()

{

        printf("Please enter your test grade.\n");

```
scanf("%d", testGrade);


if (testGrade >= 90) {

        printf("You have an A.");

}

else if (testGrade >= 80 && testGrade < 90) {

        printf("You have a B.");

}

else if (testGrade >= 70 && testGrade < 80) {

        printf("You have a C.");

}

else {

        printf("You did not receive a high enough
grade.");

}

        return 0;

}
```

Here the application requests a number; for this example, we will enter 42. The first comparison is made, but 42 is not greater than or equal to 90 so the block is skipped. The second comparison is made, but 42 is not between 80 and 90, or 70 and 80 so those blocks are also ignored. "Else" is reached, which activates when neither the if or else if statements activated, and the console prints "You did not receive a high enough grade".

When using conditional statements to make comparisons you will always start with an if statement. Else is typically the final comparison, but you can have multiple 'else if' comparisons in-between. Obviously the above code could have been written entirely with 'if' statements, but the alternative conditionals create a more readable and functional code.

Chapter 6:
More Block-Type Statements
– Loops and Switches

While

Programs written in C execute line-by-line until completion. Sometimes lines can be skipped, as we have seen with 'if exercises'. Code can be repeated continuously (which has various benefits) with looping statements as seen below.

```
int answer = 0;

printf("What is 5 x 3?\n");

while (answer != 15) {

        scanf("%d", &answer);

        if (answer != 15)

                printf("Incorrect\n");

}

Printf("Correct\n");
```

For this code the compiler asks the math question "what is 5 x 3" and then enters a while loop. So long as the answer is incorrect, the while loop will continue to run infinitely. Entering, say, 12 or 17 will display "incorrect" and then start the while loop over. Only when 15 is entered will the loop end and "correct" can be shown.

While loops have many uses such as the multiplication demonstration. They can also be used to perform iterative programming functions such as counting, waiting for input, or validating an answer while waiting for the correct one.

For

Looping can be done with other commands as well, such as the "for" loop.

```
int incNum;

for(incNum = 1; incNum <= 5; incNum++) {

    printf("%d\n", incNum);

}
```

The variable incNum is first initialized, then set to 1. The second argument of the for loop gives the condition: "so long as incNum is less than or equal to five", it will execute the next argument and everything in the block. Therefore printf() will count to 5, as it will run 5 times with incNum increasing by 1 as per the specifications. Also take note of the incNum++ statement; using double addition signs after a variable signifies to increment by one.

Switch

An astute programmer will notice that the programs above can be done just as easily with simple if statements. Loops like 'while' and 'for' accomplish tasks with less code and more simple logic, and since optimization should always be on a programmer's mind, looping statements should be used whenever possible.

Switch is another block-type statement that accomplishes the same goals as multiple ifs, but does so in a cleaner and more understandable way. For each comparison of the "switch" variable, it is matched against "cases" to determine which block of code to run.

```
printf("Enter GPA rounded to a whole number.\n);

scanf("%d", &userGPA);

switch(userGPA) {

        case 4:

                printf("You have a perfect grade\n");

                break;

        case 3:

                printf("You have honors.\n");

                break;

        case 2:

        case 1:

                printf("Try better.\n");

                break;

        default:

                printf("That doesn't seem like valid
input.\n");

        }
```

The switched variable userGPA is compared against the 5 cases provided above. If the input is 4, then it will be recognized by case 4 and the subsequent code block will run. Any time a break command is reached, the entire switch is terminated. If no break is reached, as is the situation in case 2, the program will continue to run case comparisons and code blocks until a break is reached or the curly brackets end the switch. Therefore, an input of 2 or 1 will both print "try better".

Overall, switch cases are best used when enumerating choices. One downside to them is that switches cannot use floats due to their inherent inaccuracy. An experienced programmer will be able to evaluate which situations call for switches, whiles, fors, and ifs, so they will be able to efficiently create the cleanest and most practical code.

Putting it all Together with Multiple Nested Loops

The program below demonstrates the use of nested loops, or loops that are within other loops. This program counts backwards from 5 the specified number of times and does so in a short amount of code due to the nested style. The output will be something like "5 4 3 2 1 5 4 3 2 1 5 4 3 2 1" with each on a new line.

```
// Program to demonstrate nested loops

#include <stdio.h>

int main()

{

        int firstCount, secondCount;
```

```
for (firstCount = 1; firstCount <= 3; firstCount++){

    secondCount = 5;

    while(secondCount > = 1) {

        printf("%d"\n", secondCount);

        j--;

    }

}

}
```

Chapter 7:
Intermediate C Concepts
– Pointers, File Operations

Pointers

Pointers are a confusing concept required in C-based languages. A variable stores its value in a memory address, and a pointer is a method of "pointing" to that specific address and value. In our scanf() functions involving integers, we must always use an ampersand (&) before the variable (scanf("%d", &userInput)). This is because scanf() does not change variables directly, so we have to configure it to do so by "pointing" to the value stored in userInput with &. The ampersand tells the compiler to "access the value stored in this memory location", and it thus makes the variable useful to scanf(). There are only specific functions and commands that require pointers, so a C programmer has to remember the correct times to use them. An error such as "requires type int * but was supplied int" means that the command is expecting a pointer, not a variable. File input and output requires pointers, as we will explicate below.

File Operations

Persistent programs, those that retain data even after they are closed, must write their data to a file. Upon reopening, the file must then be read to restore variables and settings. File operations refer to the input and output of data to external files.

File Output

An application can use file output functionality to create log files, save work for later, or write data to be edited by other functions and programs. In C, the first step in working with files is to create one.

FILE *fp = fopen("testfile.txt", "w");

FILE stands for the "file" data type, and fp is the typical beginner declaration name. The command fopen() attempts to read the specified "testfile.txt" with the mode set to "w" for write. Other modes can be used as well, such as "r" for reading or "r+" for both, but if w is specified and the file doesn't exist then it is created. After running the above command, testfile.txt will be created in the same directory as the compiled application.

Actually putting data into a file is done with new commands, fprintf() and fscanf(); both commands work almost identically to the ones we already know.

fprintf(fp, "Hello, World!");

Our FILE variable fp is passed as the first argument and text is passed for the second. Finally, after finishing our output operations upon a file we must close it with another command.

fclose(fp);

Failing to close a file can result in lost data or errors. After running the two commands, testfile.txt should contain our message meaning we successfully wrote to a file. Both printf() and fprintf() can also display variables and strings.

File Input

For a file input example, let us read back the contents of the testfile.txt that we created earlier. We will need to create a temporary buffer variable to store the text before it is displayed on the screen.

```
FILE *fp = fopen("testfile.txt", "r");

char inputBuffer[255];

fscanf(fp, "%s", inputBuffer);

printf("Contents of file: %s\n", inputBuffer);

fclose(fp);
```

First the file is opened in reading mode and a temporary string of large length is declared. Then fscanf() reads the first string and places it into the buffer. Finally, the contents are displayed. If you read from the file created above, the console should read "Contents of file: Hello,". Only one string of text is gathered per fscanf() execution, but loops can be used to call the entire file.

```
FILE *fp = fopen("testfile.txt", "r");

char inputBuffer[255];

int isEnd;

while (fscanf(fp, "%d", &isEnd) != EOF) {

        fscanf(fp, "%s", inputBuffer);

        printf("%s\n", inputBuffer);
```

```
        }

        fclose(fp);
```

Please note that using a loop statement like this is not always the best solution for displaying text, but it is best for getting every string from a file into memory. We use an additional variable isEnd to check for "EOF", which is the argument passed by fscanf() when the End Of File is reached. The while loop continuously displays the file string by string on new lines until EOF is read, then the program terminates. Using fgets() displays text in a console while retaining most of the formatting such as spaces, but the "while" line before it must be used to clear the input stream. The simple program below will display the "Hello, World!" line better than fscanf().

```
        FILE *fp = fopen("testfile.txt", "r");

        char inputBuffer[255];

        while (getchar() != '\n' );

        fgets(inputBuffer, 255, (FILE*)fp);

        printf("%s", inputBuffer);

        fclose(fp);
```

The fgets() command ends when EOF or the end of a line is reached, so multiple reads will require a while loop such as the one above.

Conclusively file input and output can be done with simply with the discussed commands. Basic file IO adds new features to our programming repertoire, and the process is not excessively complex. However, attention to detail regarding pointers is demanded when working with the FILE type variables.

Putting it all Together with a Simple Word Processing Program

File operations can be used to make a word processing program such as Microsoft Word. While there will not nearly be as many features, it serves as a proof of concept for a much larger project.

```
//Word processor that can store 1 line of data.

#include <stdio.h>

int main()

{

        char usrFile[255];

        int choice;

        char usrText[255];

        int isEOF;

        char inputBuffer[255];

        FILE *fp;


        printf("\n\nSimple Word Processing Application\n----------\n\n");
```

```c
        printf("Please type a filename that you want to work on: ");

        scanf("%s", usrFile);

        printf("\n\nPlease Enter 1 for editing, or 2 for viewing: ");

        scanf("%d", &choice);



        switch(choice){

                case 1:              //editing

                        fp = fopen(usrFile, "w+");  //creates file if it doesn't exist.

                        printf("\nType the contents, pressing enter to submit.\n\n");

                        while (getchar() != '\n' ); //clever hack to clear input stream

                        fgets(usrText, 255, stdin);

                        fprintf(fp, "%s", usrText);

                        fclose(fp);

                        break;

                case 2:              //viewing

                        fp = fopen(usrFile, "r");
```

```c
                if (fp == NULL){      //check to see if file
exists

                        printf("Error opening file.
Aborting.\n");

                        break;  //break if there is no file

                }

                printf("\n\n--------------Filename:%s----
----------\n", usrFile);

                while (fscanf(fp, "%d", &isEOF) != EOF) {
//keep running until EOF

                        fgets(inputBuffer, 255, (FILE*)fp);

                        printf("%s", inputBuffer);

                }

                printf("\n-----------------END OF FILE--
-----------------\n\n");

                fclose(fp);

                break;


        default:

                printf("\nThat selection is invalid.\n\n");

        }

return 0;
```

```
}
```

The word processing program can both read and create 1 line files using only commands we have learned so far. If you can break it down line-by-line and understand what is actually happening, then you are well on your way to becoming an experienced C programmer.

Chapter 8:
Other Useful C Concepts
– Structs, Functions

Structs

An array can hold multiple items of the same type, and structs can contain multiple related variables of different types. The most common use for structs is to group properties into a single record. Greater amounts of organization and tidiness arise from using structs as shown below. Structs are declared outside of the main statement.

#include <stdio.h>

#include <string.h>

```
struct student {

    char fullName[30];

    int studentID;

    char homeroom[20];

    float GPA;

};
int main(){

    struct student BHS_001;


    strcpy(BHS_001.fullName, "John Smith");
```

```
        strcpy(BHS_001.homeroom, "Mr. Jack");

        BHS_001.studentID = 2711947;

        BHS_001.GPA = 3.8;


        printf("Student record for BHS_001: %s, %s, %d, %f",
BHS_001.fullName, BHS_001.homeroom,
BHS_001.studentID, BHS_001.GPA);

        return 0;

}
```

Structs are accessed through an object-type system where struct.object references the specific variable. This is similar to arrays with array[number] giving the specific record. The printf() command accesses struct variables with the object-type reference as well.

Unions are another C feature that group together variables of differing types - very much like structs. However, we will not discuss unions in depth in this book, but nonetheless they are useful in various situations. Conclusively, structs, unions, and arrays can provide organized and in-depth records in C.

Functions

In programs we have been using the int main() function to contain all of our programs code. C only requires that one main function in a program, as that one is the function that runs by default. User-defined functions can be used to create your own custom commands, which is a great for any repeatedly called block of code. Take for instance this custom example below where we set up a function that can raise a number to a power. In it, we must use a function declaration statement outside of main() to "prototype" the parameters that we will pass. Later, we define the function's code, thus making it callable from within main().

```c
#include <stdio.h>

int powers(int powNum, int usrPow);     //prototype. 2
parameters (base and power)



int main()     //main is the only function that HAS to run

{

        int inBase, inPower;

        printf("Power Calculator-----\nPlease enter a base
number: ");

        scanf("%d", &inBase);        //get base

        printf("\nNow enter a power: ");

        scanf("%d", &inPower);       //get power


        printf("\nThe answer is : %d\n", powers(inBase,
inPower));   //call the function

        return 0;

}
```

```
int powers(int powNum, int usrPow)      //code that will run
when the function is called

{

        int count, originalIn = powNum; //set variable to keep
track of original base.

        for(count = 1; count < usrPow; count++)        //for
loop; powers are just repeated multiplication

                powNum = powNum * originalIn;       //
incremental power multiplication

        return powNum;       //return the result back to the
function

}
```

To read the above code one must realize that main() runs until
the function powers() is called. The provided parameters are
carried over into the 2nd function and operated upon. Return
is a command that finishes the function and gives the result in
the form of the variable, so the function finishes running in
main() with powNum's result returned. A simple example
such as the one above would obviously be done in shorter lines
without the custom user-defined function, but in a large
program with multiple powers() calls, it would surely save
time and data to have the extra function set up.

Chapter 9:
Additional Commands

As you increase your programming experience in C you will begin to use more preprocessor libraries and commands. Some interesting ones are listed below.

<stdio.h>	
sprintf()	Writes output to the specified string.
Sscanf()	Obtain input from a string.
fgetc()	Similar to fscanf(), but fgetc() reads from a file one character at a time.
fputc()	Puts a single character into a file.
puts()	Alternative to printf() that automatically places \n after the string.
<string.h>	
strcat()	Places the second parameter's specified string to be concatenated (added to) the first parameters' specified string.
strchr()	Searches for a specific character (first parameters) in a string (second parameters.)

strstr()	Similar to above, except it searches for a string within a string.
Strcmp()	Compares the two specified strings.
<math.h>	
sqrt()	Gives the square root of the parameter.
sin(), asin()	Gives the sin of a radian angle. Gives the arc sin in radians.
cos(), acos()	Gives the cos of a radian angle. Gives the arc cos in radians.
tan(), atan()	Gives the tan of a radian angle. Gives the arc tan in radians.
exp()	Raise the parameters to the supplied exponent.
log()	Returns the natural log of the parameter.
fabs()	Gives the absolute value of the parameter.
<time.h>	
time_t time	Encodes time into the provided string. See example below for usage.

rand()	Create a pseudo random number from o to MAX.

Putting Everything Together for a Final Program

//This is a program that aims to be a personal planner. It uses commands and the smaller programs throughout this book to achieve a variety of tasks.

```
#include <stdio.h>

#include <math.h>

#include <string.h>

#include <time.h>


int main(void)

{

    FILE *fp;

    FILE *fp2;

    char usrName[30];

    char inputBuffer[255];

    char buffName[255];

    int choice;
```

```c
time_t rawtime;

struct tm * timeinfo;

int cont = 1;

int tmp;



while (cont = 1)          //this    while    loop    exists    to
continuously loop the program

{

fp = fopen("intlog.txt", "r");    //attempt    to    load    the
program data

if (fp == NULL){          //if it doesn't exist, create it

        printf("Program    not    installed...    Running
initialization.\n\n");

    printf("What is your name? ");

    fgets(usrName, 30, stdin);

    printf("\n\nInstalling...\n\n\n");

    fp = fopen("intlog.txt", "w");

    fprintf(fp, "%s", usrName);

    fclose(fp);

    printf("Program initialized. Please run again for full
functionality.\n\n");
```

```
    return 1;

}


Else //if it does exist, load the program like normal

{

    fgets(buffName, 255, (FILE*)fp);    //load user name in
to variable

    fp2 = fopen("memo.txt", "r");


    if (fp2 == NULL)

        printf("\n\nWelcome back, %sWhat would you like to
do?\n\n", buffName);        //no memo

    else

    {

        fgets(inputBuffer, 255, (FILE*)fp2);

        printf("\n\nWelcome back, %s%s\n\n", buffName,
inputBuffer);//with memo

    }

    printf("1: View time and date\n");  //display        menu
options

    printf("2: Calculator\n");
```

```c
if (fp2 == NULL)

    printf("3: Leave myself a note\n");

else{

    printf("3: Delete my note\n");

    fclose(fp2);

}

printf("4: Magic 8 Ball \n");

printf("5: About\n");

printf("6: Uninstall\n");

printf("7: Quit\n\n");


fclose(fp);


scanf("%d", &choice);


switch (choice){

    case 1:

        time(&rawtime);

        timeinfo = localtime(&rawtime);        //gets time
```

```c
        printf("\n\nToday's date and time is: %s\n\n",
asctime (timeinfo));

        break;

    case 2:

        printf("\n\nPlease select function: \n\n");

        printf("1: Addition\n");

        printf("2: Subtraction\n");

        printf("3: Multiplication\n");

        printf("4: Division\n\n");

        int mathchoice;

        scanf("%d", &mathchoice);

        float firstNum, secondNum, calcAnswer;

        printf("\n\nEnter first number: ");

        scanf("%f", &firstNum);

        printf("\nEnter second number: ");

        scanf("%f", &secondNum);

        switch (mathchoice) {

            case 1:

                calcAnswer = firstNum + secondNum;
```

```
        break;
    case 2:
        calcAnswer = firstNum - secondNum;
        break;
    case 3:
        calcAnswer = firstNum * secondNum;
        break;
    case 4:
        calcAnswer = firstNum / secondNum;
        break;
    default:
        printf("\nInvalid\n\n");
    }


    printf("Answer is %f\n\n", calcAnswer);
    break;
case 3:
    if (fp2 != NULL)
    remove("memo.txt");
```

```c
        else {

            char usrMemo[55];

            printf("\n\nEnter the reminder's text: ");

            while (getchar() != '\n');

            fgets(usrMemo, 55, stdin);              //same      as
word processing program earlier

            fp2 = fopen("memo.txt", "w");

            fprintf(fp2, "%s", usrMemo);

            fclose(fp2);

        }

        break;

    case 4:

        srand(time(NULL));

        int r = rand() % 3 + 1;    //funny    trick   to   get   a
random number from 1 to 4


        switch(r){

            case 1:

                printf("Yes.\n");

                break;
```

```c
        case 2:

            printf("No.\n");

            break;

        case 3:

            printf("Maybe.\n");

            break;

        default:

            printf("Ask again...\n");


        }

        break;

    case 5:

        printf("\n\nThis is the final project from the programming book on C.\n");

        printf("This project is a culmination of many skills learned so far.\n");

        printf("Successfully getting this program to work means I have learned the basics of C.\n\n");

        break;

    case 6:

        remove("memo.txt");
```

```
        remove("intlog.txt");

                printf("\n\nFiles   deleted.   Program
uninstalled. Aborting.\n");

        return 3;

      default:

        return 2;



    }



  }



}       //loop back

  return 0;

}
```

The program has multiple functions all placed within the same program through nested case statements. Ultimately the above program is only large because it contains many features that are broken up into smaller subroutines. The code could very much be more organized by using custom functions, but that is your homework for another time if you wish to take the challenge!

Chapter 10:
More Considerations

Best Programming Practices

Programming in C does not require readability and neatness-only functionality is necessary. Despite this, there are still a few best programming practices that every programmer should follow to help both themselves and any other person that might have to read the code.

Using Comments

Comments are a helpful reminder of what the code is doing at certain points in the program. Uncommented code can often be incomprehensive to anybody but the original writer, so any programs that involve a team of multiple programmers need to be documented precisely. Furthermore, even solo projects can become complex and unwieldy without annotations to serve as guideposts and reminders.

Additionally, documenting meta-specifics of code such as the creation date, authors, and general purpose through comments is a fantastic way to save time. For example, a new programmer might open "important.c" and read the top line *"//Important.c is used to shutdown the server before it gets too hot. Keep running at all times. Written by Jack Smith and last edited on August 12th, 2014. "*. The new programmer instantly knows the entire purpose of the code from only the top line and react accordingly.

Indented Code

Giant blocks of text are highly unreadable in programming. Indenting code refers to the act of offsetting related lines of text. Refer to the following:

```
int main() {

    int userInput;

    scanf("%d", userInput);


    if (userInput > 1000) {

        printf("Large number.");

    }

    else {

        printf("Small number.");

    }

    return 0;

}
```

Instantly the code conveys where certain sections contain their boundaries. Everything is part of main, but only certain commands are in the "if" section. The indentation method used above (and throughout the book) is the tab method, where each further level of code is tabbed in another space. Some users prefer using spaces instead to keep the white space to a minimum. C eliminates any white space when compiling anyways, so it doesn't matter whether you tab, space, or refuse to indent at all. But overall, organizing code through separation of scope results in a readable and understandable arrangement.

Descriptive Variable Names

Beginning programmers usually continue using their first variable names – var1, name, input, etc... While great for examples and small programs, rudimentary variable names often do more harm to the programmer than they realize. Var1 is meaningless without context, so unless the code is commented every time var1 appears than readers will quickly forget what it is supposed to represent. Combat this with descriptive variable names such as firstName, interestAmount, or dollarsEarned. The more expressive a variable name is the more likely it is instantly recognizable.

Simplicity

Coders strive for the most "elegant" solution to a problem. Elegant is a programming term referring to a clean, clever, and functional solution to a programming problem. Just because a piece of program works does not always mean the best code has been implemented. Some programmers continue using simple and rudimentary commands rather than the more difficultly understood ones, and program efficiency is lost as a result. Strive to create "simple" programs in terms of brevity, elegance, and functionality rather than "easy" simple. Combine all of the above tips to create an attractively designed source code that will make less-inclined programmers jealous.

Optimization

Code can be optimized in different ways. Some commands may run faster than others, and some may take up less resources. Which way a programmer optimizes his code is up to the goals of the project, but there should always be some optimizing taking place as the programmer is writing. The programs in this book were only optimized for programmer readability; you can get some optimization practice by redoing the code to be smaller or faster.

What to Learn Next

Most people learn C as their first language to get a decent understanding of how programming works in general. As C is the root of many languages, you may now notice that other programming languages seem similar in many ways. It is recommended that you continue learning C functions or branch out and learn other programming languages as well.

Some individuals learn programming to get into video game development. C can certainly help you there, as there are some user-created libraries focused on game development such as Allegro 5. After downloading the libraries (http://liballeg.org/download.html), you can follow some of the tutorials (https://wiki.allegro.cc/index.php?title=Getting_Started) on how to integrate the libraries into your C development workflow. A basic understanding of C is quite necessary to operate these types of development tools - as most assume that you have a decent grasp of how C works. Once you have the libraries installed, you can link the preprocessor statements into your projects and begin using new functions that can draw on the screen and create animations.

No matter what you wish for your next step to be, definitely continue learning programming and increasing your skills. Skilled programmers are always in high demand and jobs will only open up as time goes on and more aspects of our lives are integrated with technology.

Addendum - Keywords in C

C89 has multiple keywords (also known as reversed words) that cannot be used as variable names, types, functions, or anything other than what their purpose is for. They are listed below.

auto	break	case
Char	const	continue
default	do	double
Else	enum	extern
float	for	goto
if	int	long
register	return	short
signed	sizeof	static
struct	switch	typedef
union	void	volatile
while		

The C99 added five more keywords.

_Bool	_Complex	_Imaginary
inline	restrict	

C11 added even more keywords.

_Alignas	_Atomic	_Generic
_Noreturn	_Static_assert	_Thread_local

Addendum – Advanced C Concepts to Research

So far we have been letting the compiler set aside memory locations for us automatically. Furthermore, when declaring strings of variable length, we have been setting the array to a high value such as 255. This is not the most efficient way of doing this, because we can have truly dynamically sized memory allocation by doing it manually with malloc(), calloc(), and realloc().

Minute memory management continues to be advantageous with the free() command, which frees up a memory location that isn't needed anymore, thus making execution faster and more efficient.

Recursion is a feature within lower-level programming languages that allows functions to call themselves. It is done by simply calling the current function while operating within it. Practical uses come from operations requiring multiple iterations, such as the power function we wrote earlier.

Networking in C is a difficult process, but figuring out how it works will imbue you with advanced networking and C knowledge. With more preprocessor statements such as <sys/socket.h> and <netinet/in.h>, we can write code that initializes "sockets" to handle the flow of network data. TCP and UDP are used alongside internet addresses just as in normal networking, and sockets are used to gather the networking data that is sent between two clients. For networking programming, you will need two computers that can run C code, because you need to have one act as the sender and one be the receiver.

There are other extremely advanced programming topics that this book cannot discuss in a short amount of time. Doing research and completing programming challenges will only help your understanding of programming languages.

Conclusion

Thanks again for taking the time to read this book!

You should now have a good understanding of C Programming and be able to do some basic C Programming! I hope that this beginner's guide has served you well, and opened your mind up to what's possible with programming!

If you enjoyed this book, please take the time to leave me a review on Amazon. I appreciate your honest feedback, and it really helps me to continue producing high quality books.